For My lovely
Nanna.

Happy Birthd[a]

With lots of love

Clare
xxx.

WEXFORD
THEN & NOW

JARLATH GLYNN

COLOUR PHOTOGRAPHY BY PÁDRAIG GRANT

The
History
Press
Ireland

In memory of my parents
Michael and Helena Glynn

First published 2013

The History Press Ireland
50 City Quay
Dublin 2
Ireland
www.thehistorypress.ie

© Jarlath Glynn, 2013

The right of Jarlath Glynn to be identified as the Author
of this work has been asserted in accordance with the
Copyrights, Designs and Patents Act 1988.

British Library Cataloguing in Publication Data.
A catalogue record for this book is available from the British Library.

ISBN 978 1 84588 805 3

Typesetting and origination by The History Press

CONTENTS

ACKNOWLEDGEMENTS

I would like to acknowledge all those who helped me during the production of this book. In particular, my colleague Pádraig Grant who took all the modern photographs. I would especially like to thank those who allowed me to use photographs from their own collections: An tAthair Séamus S De Vál, John Hayes, Michael Kavanagh, Dominic Kiernan Denise O'Connor Murphy and James and Sylvia O'Connor. Also Keith Murphy from the National Library. I am indebted to my library colleague Celestine Rafferty and to John Furlong for helpful advice. To my publisher Ronan Colgan many thanks for his patience and professionalism.

To all the owners of premises which feature in the book and to the following who helped in various ways during the course of my research: Bernard Browne, Mairead Coleman, the late Billy Colfer, Peggy Connolly, Brian and Francis Coulter, Monica Crofton, the late Michael Curran, Paddy Donovan, Gráinne Doran, Nicky Furlong, Liam Gaul, Revd Matt Glynn, Sr Siobhan Hayden, Adrian Haythornthwaite, Ken Hemingway, Peter Hussey, David McLoughlin, Hilary Murphy, Michael Murphy, Robert O'Callaghan, James G. and Paula O'Connor, Jack O'Leary, Dr Austin O'Sullivan, Peter Pearson, Suzanne Power, Nicky Rossiter, David Rowe, Eithne Scallan, Ernie Shepherd and Matt Wheeler.

I should especially like to thank my wife Louisa and children, Emma and Conor, for their support and patience while I was researching and writing this book.

ABOUT THE AUTHOR & PHOTOGRAPHER

Jarlath Glynn is a librarian and local historian. He has had a life-long interest in the history of his native town and county. He has lectured, written about, and conducted tours of County Wexford. A member of Wexford Historical Society since the early 1980s, he has served it in various roles and is currently president of the society.

Pádraig Grant is an internationally exhibited and award-winning photographer. Born in Wexford in 1967, his work has taken him to the four corners of the world.

Previous publications include; *African Shadows* (1995), *A Remarkable Festival* (2001), *With This, or Upon This* (2007) as well as two limited edition handmade books featuring photographs of the Wexford coastline *The Beach Day* (2010) and *25, Direct/Reflect* (2012).

More of his work can be seen at his fine art photographic gallery, The Rowe Street Gallery in Wexford or online at www.padraiggrant.com.

INTRODUCTION

Wexford is a town of great character and individuality formed by its physical location and its complex mix of various ethnic groups. Defining historical events, such as the Cromwellian occupation of the town, the 1798 rebellion and the 1911 industrial dispute, have all shaped the personality of the town while ecclesiastical and industrial expansion in the nineteenth and twentieth centuries have left a lasting imprint on its architecture. The strategic importance of Wexford Port and the constant human traffic in and out of the town have led to an outward-looking view of the world among its inhabitants.

This book concentrates on the physical environment, the buildings and streetscapes of the town. Most of the original black and white photographs date from around 1900; some are much later. The subject matter of the photographs dates from medieval times to the present day. They were chosen to reflect the varied and diverse aspects of the history of the town. The sites identified illustrate what has survived and what has not. The text attempts to link the past to the present and to tell the story of what happened in between.

The majority of buildings and streetscapes featured are still in existence and have changed little, such as the medieval street pattern and laneways, sections of the town wall, the 'Twin Churches' (see pp. 78-81), the Franciscan Friary, St Peter's College, to mention but a few. Other buildings have been adapted to fulfil a different role. The nineteenth-century quay front, reminiscent of a New England whaling town with its distinctive wooden works, has been replaced by a modern amenity area, and the Theatre Royal, the home of Wexford Festival Opera, has been replaced by a striking new opera house which dominates the Wexford skyline. Some very important buildings such as Pierce's Iron Works, Bishopswater Distillery, Wexford Courthouse, the Mercy Convent, White's Hotel and two Wexford bridges have disappeared. Some sites have been sensitively restored: Westgate tower and sections of the town wall are good examples. The Bullring and the Redmond monument have also been refurbished in keeping with the original plans for both squares. Whether some other recent developments are in keeping with the architecture of the historic town is debatable.

About twelve of the photographs in this book can be credited to Robert French, the chief outdoor photographer of the William Lawrence Studios in Dublin. They were taken between 1880 and 1914. His collection of over 19,000 prints is housed in the National Photographic Archive in Temple Bar, Dublin which is part of the National Library of Ireland. Other photographs come from private collections and have not been published before. Six of the photographs come from glass plates which were discovered in a house in Dublin and rescued by a Wexford historian. The photographer is unknown. Several photographs were taken by Mr John Scanlon, a member of Wexford Historical Society, who captured many views of Wexford town in the 1940s, '50s and '60s. Other views were taken by Michael Kavanagh. All the modern colour photographs were taken by Pádraig Grant.

ADORATION CONVENT/ CHRISTIAN BROTHERS

THE COMMUNITY OF nuns who live in this convent belong to an enclosed order devoted to prayer and the veneration of the Eucharist. Attached to Bride Street parochial church, prayer takes place in the church during the day and in the convent chapel at night. In recent years, due to declining numbers, lay people have assisted the nuns in maintaining adoration.

The foundation of the community came about in 1870, when the then bishop, Dr Thomas Furlong (1803-1875), requested the Sisterhood of Marie Reparatrice establish a

branch of their order in Wexford. Out of this community evolved a uniquely Wexford-based order in 1875. From that date adoration has continued. The convent moved to its present location in 1887 from Rockfield on Newtown Road. The philanthropist Richard Devereux contributed towards the cost of the new building and it was built by Mary O'Connor, a local builder. It is considered to be one of the finest buildings in the town, combining red sandstone and granite on the outside and beautiful wood carving inside. *(Image from the Lawrence Collection, courtesy of the National Library of Ireland)*

ORIGINALLY THERE WERE thirty-eight nuns in the community. Today there are ten. The community continues its work and is an oasis of quiet reflection in the town.

The building in the right foreground of the photograph is the monastery of the Christian Brothers community, dating from 1873.

Almost a decade before the building of the 'Twin Churches' (see pp. 78-81), the Christian Brothers opened their first school in the Faythe in 1849. In 1853, a school in George's Street built by the people of the town in memory of their parish priest, Dr John Sinnott, was opened. This school remained open until 1971, when the pupils transferred to the present location on Green Street.

When the monastery was built in Joseph Street in 1873 a school with four classrooms was erected behind it. In 1939, a completely new primary school was opened in Green Street. Over the years the secondary and primary schools have been enlarged and refurbished to cater for increasing numbers of pupils.

Today, the primary school has 250 pupils and the secondary school has 550 pupils. Ten retired Christian Brothers live in the monastery.

ANNE STREET

THIS STREET WAS most likely named after Queen Anne (1665-1714) and until the early eighteenth century the sea would have come as far as a steep cliff at the top of the street. Three buildings of significance appear in this photograph. On the right is the three-storey post office with redbrick frontage. The post office underwent a major renovation in 1987 and was reroofed in 1993, which did not enhance the original design of the building.

Clad in ivy and adjacent to the post office is the Presbyterian church which was built in 1843. It was designed and constructed by Thomas Willis who was also the architect and builder of the Methodist chapel in Row Street (1835) and St Ibar's church in Castlebridge (1855). The Anne Street church walls are built of red sandstone from Park and a Tudor-headed latticed lancet window can be seen over the main door. The church design is very simple with only the slightest architectural embellishments.

At the top of the street, on the right, one can just decipher the first four letters of the Mechanics Institute. It was built in 1859 by Edwin Thomas Willis. The building diminishes in scale as you look upwards to the top of the building. On the roof is a hexagonal glass construction which would have given a commanding view of shipping in Wexford Harbour. The objective of the Institute was to educate young men in the arts, sciences and general literature. This was achieved by providing a library, reading room, classes and occasional lectures. A committee of leading businessmen, landowners and clergy ran the club. *(Image from the Michael Kavanagh collection courtesy of Michael Kavanagh)*

THE GENERAL POST office and Presbyterian church have changed little over the years except for minor alterations. The Mechanics Institute closed in the 1930s and is now empty, with only the ground floor being used for retail purposes.

BATT STREET

THIS STREET, LEADING down to the harbour, has long been associated with fishermen. It was named after Jane Batt, an extensive property owner in the town in the nineteenth century, who owned several houses in this street. Members of the Batt family are buried near Taghmon where an obelisk was erected to their memory.

The Lett family has been involved in the export of fresh mussels, farmed in Wexford Harbour, since the nineteenth century and their thriving business was located here

until 2000. Their business expanded rapidly from the mid-1960s and by 1990 it had 365 employees. The Letts were pioneers in the mussel fishing industry and their Tuskar Rock brand of seafood products was exported worldwide from the late 1970s. Currently, the company is involved solely in the export of mussels to Europe from Wexford Harbour, which is now a European Designated Shellfish Harbour.

Batt Street also supported other businesses. There was a thriving poultry export business in the years after the First World War and in the 1940s the Slaney Mineral Water Company Water operated out of Batt Street exporting its products throughout Ireland. *(Image from the John Scanlon collection courtesy of Dominic Kiernan)*

THE GOOD TIDE Harbour development at the end of the street was built by the Lett family. It is on both sides of the street and comprises seventy-three apartments. The yellow brick building on the left of the photograph shows public housing built by Wexford Borough Council in 2005.

BISHOP'S HOUSE

BISHOP'S HOUSE IS most likely an eighteenth-century house later enlarged and adapted in the nineteenth century. In the left-hand side of the photograph the façade facing the town is a later addition. In 1785, the house was sold by the Hattons to the Suttons, both prominent Wexford landed families. In turn, it was sold by the Suttons to a branch of the Talbots, a very influential and wealthy Catholic family. Later, members of the Redmond family occupied the house until 1847 after which the Devereux family of Wexford Distillery took up residence. In the 1860s, the Devereux family bought the house and land. Despite popular belief, Nicholas's brother, the businessman Richard Devereux, never lived there

and resided instead in South Main Street. In 1868-69, Mary Francis Devereux transferred the property to a diocesan trust.

Bishop Codd (1918-1938) was the first bishop to reside here. Bishop James Browne (1884-1918), his predecessor, had lived in St Mary's, a property beside the present Bishop's House and now the Wexford School of Music. From the mid-seventeenth century onwards the Bishop of Ferns has usually resided in Wexford town. A change came with Bishop Patrick Ryan (1814-1819) who moved residence to Enniscorthy where he initiated the building of St Aidan's Cathedral and, also, St Peter's College in Wexford. Both his successors, Bishops Keating and Murphy, lived in Enniscorthy. Bishop Thomas Furlong (1857-1875), probably the most important Bishop of Ferns in the nineteenth century, lived in St Peter's College. His successor, Michael Warren (1876-1884), moved back to Enniscorthy and was succeeded by James Browne who moved to St Mary's, Summerhill in 1884. Successive Bishops of Ferns have lived in Wexford town ever since. *(Image courtesy of An tAthair Séamus S de Vál)*

TODAY, THE HOUSE is the residence of Bishop Denis Brennan. It also serves as the administrative headquarters of the Diocese of Ferns.

BISHOPSWATER
DISTILLERY

THIS LARGE COMPLEX of buildings, now long disappeared, on Distillery Road was the
Bishopswater Distillery. Nicholas Devereux, who established the distillery in 1827, came
from a famous Wexford merchant family. The history and development of the Devereux
family runs parallel to the development of the church and the economy of Wexford town
in the nineteenth century.

 The distillery was built by a consortium of local businessmen at a cost of £30,000 and
traded as Devereux and Harvey. In 1833, Nicholas Devereux became the sole proprietor.

The buildings were substantial and built of local stone, with three large brick chimneys, and a large water-wheel provided power. It is recorded that in 1833 Devereux paid duty on 200,000 gallons of whiskey. Nicholas Devereux died in 1840 and was succeeded by his son, Richard. During the Great Famine of 1847 Richard Devereux closed the stills to ensure that grain was used for food. In 1886, the distillery was producing 110,000 gallons a year and was described as being on a six-acre site with a 582ft frontage and employing seventy men.

The distillery was successful but never grew large enough to compete with the Dublin distilleries. It ran into difficulties in the early 1900s and distilling ceased in 1914. In 1930, Pierce Engineering purchased the buildings and operated successfully as a bicycle factory but closed in 1940. The last of the complex of buildings was demolished in the 1970s. *(Image courtesy of An tAthair Séamus S de Vál)*

ALL THAT REMAINS of the distillery now is the original entrance gate with the words Casa Rio (River House) above it in wrought iron. This gate can be seen in the right-hand corner of the original photograph. Pierce's built a terrace of redbrick housing for some of its workers along the street frontage of the old distillery.

CHURCH LANE

LANEWAYS ARE AN integral part of the historical development of Wexford. In a recent article local historian, Nicholas Rossiter, identified over seventy laneways that had existed in the town. Church Lane can be identified from the eighteenth century. Some of the other lanes date back over 1,000 years. The construction of the quay in the early nineteenth century led to the decline of the laneways which had been used for centuries to gain access to the port. In recent times there is no longer access to many of the laneways.

The substantial property on the left of the photograph attached to the graveyard was the townhouse of the Marquis of Ely of Loftus Hall. He was a prominent politician and Mayor of Wexford in 1793. Ely House at the end of Wexford bridge was named after him. The house in Church Lane was later to become the Workingmen's Society, one of many similar facilities

in the town. Another benefit society was located on the right-hand side of the laneway called the Wexford branch of the Irish National Foresters. It was founded in 1877 to support Irish nationalism and by 1914 it had a quarter of a million members worldwide. Other businesses existed in this laneway. The proprietor of the business on the right-hand side of the photograph was Matthew Harpur and the sign over the door reads 'Matthew Harpur Manure and Implement Depot'. He also owned premises close by at Nos 23 and 28 North Main Street, selling a wide range of hardware products. The doorway in the wall of St Iberius leads to a graveyard. Only three headstones survive but it is almost certain that others were buried in the vicinity of the church. *(Image courtesy of An tAthair Séamus S de Vál)*

ORIGINALLY THE LANEWAY ran directly to the quay front. In recent decades almost all of the laneway has been opened up to cater for business, office and residential development.

COMMODORE JOHN BARRY STATUE

THE PLINTH UNDER construction at Crescent Quay in this 1956 photograph is for a bronze statue of John Barry presented by the American people to the people of Ireland. The monument was designed by the American sculptor Wheeler Williams. In the United States there are two other statues of Barry, one in front of Independence Hall in Philadelphia and the other in Franklin Square, Washington.

Barry had quite a remarkable career. He came from a seafaring family in the vicinity of Tacumshane and was born in the mid-1740s. He left home at the age of fourteen for Philadelphia where he more than likely had family connections. Starting as a cabin boy,

he quickly rose through the ranks to the highest command. He commanded his first ship, the *Barbados*, in his early twenties. With the outbreak of the War of Independence he was given command, at the age of thirty-one, of the warship *Lexington*. He commanded a number of Continental Navy ships during the war.

Barry returned to maritime trading after the war. He sailed from Philadelphia to the Orient. He was a good friend of George Washington and was appointed senior captain in the US Navy. Between 1798 and 1801 he directed American Operations in the West Indies. He was squadron leader of the fleet until his early death in 1803. Because of his exceptional contribution to the American Navy he was conferred with the title 'the Father of the American Navy' in 1895. He died on 13 September 1803 at the age of fifty-eight and was given a full military funeral and is buried in St Mary's cemetery Philadelphia. *(Image from the Denis O'Connor collection courtesy of Denise O'Connor Murphy)*

TWO AMERICAN PRESIDENTS have visited the Barry Memorial. Most famous was the visit of John F. Kennedy to the town on 27 June 1963. A year earlier, on 23 August 1962, General Dwight D. Eisenhower had laid a wreath at Crescent Quay. He had served two terms in office, retiring in 1961.

Four United States Navy destroyers have been named after Barry. The current USS *Barry*, commissioned in 1992, has Norfolk, Virginia as its home port. The previous USS *Barry*, decommissioned in 1982, is now a museum ship at the Washington Navy Yard.

CORNMARKET

IT IS UNCERTAIN how early a market existed here but Cornmarket would have marked the northern boundary of the Norse town. Entry to the town for the purpose of trade was through St John's Gate. The Normans developed the market and introduced strict laws that goods could only be sold in Cornmarket.

The Market House, better known as the Assembly Rooms, was built in 1775. It was a major addition to the architecture of the town. On the ground floor there were open arches for trading and above it was a ballroom with ornate plastering, while adjacent to this was a supper room. These were used by many of the landed families who had town houses in the vicinity. On the demolition of the Court House, the Corporation built the Tholsel in the Bullring in 1794. It had a council chamber, offices for the mayor and town clerk, a court of conscience on the first floor and a fish market underneath. It was demolished in 1898 and the Assembly Rooms became the home of the Corporation until they moved to the old Tate school in 1949.

Other buildings of note include the Thomas Moore Tavern and Kelly's of Cornmarket. Kelly's, which incorporated five older shops, also housed an independent church called Bethesda. Later, it became a theatre until it closed in 1832. *(Image from the Lawrence collection courtesy of the National Library of Ireland)*

THE OLD MARKET House was converted into Wexford Arts Centre in 1974. Since then it has provided a wide range of cultural activities including theatre, music, dance, and exhibitions for the people of the town. The striking modern building in the centre of the photograph is the new County Library which opened in November 2012. Designed by Architect James O'Leary, it houses a wide range of services over three floors.

COUNTY HALL

THIS IS A close-up of what was the entrance to Wexford Jail from 1840 having replaced an earlier, simpler gateway. The jail was designed by Sir Richard Morrison and built by Wexford Grand Jury in 1807-1808. Morrison also designed the Courthouse at Commercial Quay. The jail had a large complex of buildings. All that remains today is the female prison (largely intact with cells), a perimeter wall and the frontage at the main entrance. It ceased being a jail in 1904 and was formally handed over to Wexford County Council in 1905. The St John of God community ran it as a centre for 'inebriate women' until 1920 when it was handed back to the County Council and until very recently served as their offices.

The building is first recorded as County Hall when the Council met there on 7 October 1920. In the following turbulent years it had to vacate the premises for the Royal Irish Constabulary who used it as a barracks in 1921. The Free State army requisitioned the premises in 1923-1924. On 13 March 1923 three Republicans, James Parle (Taghmon), Patrick Hogan (Wexford) and John Creane (Taghmon) were executed by firing squad in the yard behind the old jail. Today there is a garden of remembrance accessible from Hill Street on the site. *(Image courtesy of An tAthair Séamus S de Vál)*

IT WAS DECIDED in 2005 to construct new council offices at Carricklawn, just outside the town. The new headquarters was designed by Robin Lee, architects, in association with Arthur Gibney and partners. It was named the best public building in Ireland by the Royal Institute of Architects of Ireland. Previously, it was shortlisted for the World Building of the Year award.

ELY HOUSE

THIS PHOTOGRAPH SHOWS a fine Georgian house
that was demolished in 1975 to make way for a new
hospital. The name of the house owes its origins to
the Marquis of Ely of Loftus Hall. He was Mayor of
Wexford in 1793 and he had considerable political
influence which was only eclipsed by Catholic
Emancipation in 1829.

Ely House passed from the Hughes family to
the Doran family in the mid-nineteenth century.
It continued to be owned by the Doran family until
1943. During the First World War, large numbers
of allied ships were sunk by German U boats off the
Wexford coast and to counter these naval attacks
Wexford was chosen by the United States Navy as
a base for a squadron of sea planes to patrol the
southeast coast and destroy German submarines. In a
very short time the shipping lanes around Tuskar Rock
were cleared of submarines.

The naval base was built just north of Ely House and
the house itself served as the officers' residence. By 1918
there were twenty officers and 406 other personnel.

The base was extensive and photographs of the time show four aircraft hangers and numerous rows of wooden housing and offices. All that remains today of the naval base is a concrete slip opposite Ferrybank Motors where the sea planes were launched into Wexford Harbour. *(Image courtesy of An tAthair Séamus S de Vál)*

THE AMERICANS DEPARTED in 1919, the base having been dismantled and auctioned. In 1944, Ely House (property and lands) was purchased by the religious Order of St John of God who established a nursing home there. The building of a new hospital was completed in 1975.

GEORGE'S STREET

GEORGE'S STREET IS probably named after St George rather than a monarch. It may date as far back as the fourteenth century as St George was venerated at that time. However, the first mention of the street is in 1666. The most striking feature of Lower George's Street is the substantial Georgian houses. This early photograph gives us some idea of what the town houses of the ascendancy looked like. Landed families in the county built these houses for social and political reasons and similar houses can still be seen in Monck Street and Main Street. High-profile families such as the Harveys of Bargy Castle and the Colcloughs of Tintern Abbey lived on this street. Both families were to play a prominent role in the 1798 rebellion. Beauchamp Bagenal Harvey, one of the leaders of the rebellion, was hanged close by on Wexford bridge. Just around the corner in Trimmer's Lane was the residence of Esmond Kyan, Commander of Artillery in 1798.

To the left of the lady in the photograph was the Colcloughs' town house. It was here that the wake of John Coclough took place in 1807. He was killed in a duel with William Congreve Alcock of Wilton Castle at Ardcandrisk. It was said that Colclough's funeral procession to Tintern was one of the largest ever seen in County Wexford. On this site was the residence of Dr Tom Walsh, founder of Wexford Festival Opera. Several legal practices, including M.J. O'Connor, did business here. *(Image from the Michael Kavanagh collection courtesy of Michael Kavanagh)*

THESE FINE GEORGIAN houses are still intact though they are now mainly used for business premises or apartments. The street declined in importance in the 1900s but in recent years there has been some redevelopment of the area.

GLENA TERRACE

THIS ELEGANT TERRACE of eight redbrick three-storey houses was built in 1892 by the noted builder Mary O'Connor (1837-1927). On the early death of her husband she took over his building practice and in the following years was to make a significant contribution to the architecture of Wexford town. The first house on Glena Terrace was built for the solicitor M.J. O'Connor. In 1894, Mary O'Connor also built the first purpose-built solicitor's offices in Ireland for M.J. O'Connor at the corner of Lower George's Street and Selskar Street.

In little over a decade her output of buildings was impressive. In proximity to Glena Terrace she constructed two private dwellings, Ard Ruadh (1893) and Clifton (1895), for prominent citizens. Earlier she had built a fine terrace of houses in Upper George's Street. Her most outstanding building is the Convent of the Sisters of Perpetual Adoration beside Bride Street church. She also constructed the chapel in the St John of God Convent, Newtown Road. One of the characteristics of her work was that she put the date of building on some of her work. Many of her buildings were built in redbrick, sandstone and decorated with granite and were characterised by excellent workmanship. *(Image from the Lawrence collection courtesy of the National Library of Ireland)*

DOWN THROUGH THE years many prominent citizens have lived in Glena Terrace, among them Eugene McCarthy, the owner of White's Hotel. The parents of the author John Brennan (pseudonym John Welcome) also lived here. Over the last number of years with the passage of time some of the brick work façades have had to be refurbished but the terrace retains its original charm.

JOHN'S GATE STREET

THE STREET DERIVED its name from the medieval gateway which was in the centre of the street as we see here. It was connected on both sides to the town wall. There were six other medieval gateways in the town. Entry to town for the purposes of trade was through St John's Gate as the Cornmarket was situated just south of it. Due to the increased volume of traffic from surrounding areas the tower and gate were removed in the early nineteenth century.

The graveyard at the very top of the street, St John's, was the site of a medieval church. It was a church of the Knights Hospitallers, dating from the late twelfth century. No remnant of the building survives but a thirteenth-century upright stone coffin is evidence of the antiquity of the site. The central focus of the graveyard is a large Gothic-style cut-granite mausoleum with cast-iron doors and metal pinnacles on the roof. It is the final resting place of John Edward

Redmond (1856-1918), the leader of the Irish Parliamentary Party. Many members of the prominent Wexford families the Talbots and the Redmonds are buried in the mausoleum. It was built by John Hyacinth Talbot (1793-1868) in memory of his wife, Anne Eliza Redmond (1799-1826), who died at the age of twenty-seven. The mausoleum was built in 1828, at a cost of £900. The graveyard is also the resting place of Richard Monaghan, also known as 'Dick Monk' (d. 1798) a captain of the United Irish insurgents who fought at the Battle of Arklow in 1798. *(Image from the John Scanlon collection courtesy of Dominic Kiernan)*

THE STREETSCAPE HAS not changed much since the original photograph was taken. A large house slightly out of view on the right-hand side of the street was built in the 1780s and is now the Blue Egg Gallery, opened in October 2011. On the left-hand side of the street is housing from the 1970s.

MERCY CONVENT

THIS LARGE COMPLEX of buildings in Summerhill at the rear of St Peter's College was the Mercy Convent. The convent and chapel are to the right with the school in the centre and the large building on the far left is an orphanage

The convent was founded in 1840, when the nuns took up residence in a small house on the quay. In 1842, they took over the orphanage that had been established by the Redmond and Talbot families. Wealthy merchant Richard Devereux provided the funds for the building of the new convent and school and also financed another school in George's Street in 1858. This school continued until 1945, when it transferred to its present location on St John's Road. In 1865, Devereux also endowed a 'House of Mercy' attached to the Mercy Convent for the 'training of orphan girls as servants, and as a place for them when out of employment'. The orphanage closed in the 1970s.

As well as the Sisters of Mercy and the Christian Brothers other religious orders, namely the Presentation Sisters (1818), the St John of God Sisters (1873) and the Loreto Sisters (1866), provided much-needed educational institutions. This was made possible by a wealthy merchant class in the town. *(Image courtesy of An tAthair Séamus S de Vál)*

THE PRIMARY SCHOOL shown in the photograph relocated to Kennedy Park in 1973 and the nuns moved to a modern convent in Clonard when the Summerhill complex of buildings was demolished in 1985. The site is now a housing estate. Buildings such

as the Convent of Mercy fundamentally changed the character of the town and the disappearance of this complex of buildings is a reminder of the decline in importance of such institutions.

M.J. O'CONNOR AND COMPANY, SOLICITORS

THIS SPLENDID TWO-STOREY redbrick property with yellow-brick corner stones was built by Mary O'Connor in 1888 for M.J. O'Connor. It stands on the site of a townhouse reputed to have been owned by Bagenal Harvey of Bargy Castle, one of the main leaders of the

1798 rebellion. The founder of the firm was not only a brilliant solicitor but also a keen sportsman, philanthropist and reformer. His writings in the newspaper the *Freeman's Journal* inspired the Secretary of State for Ireland, George Wyndham, to present the Wyndham Land Act to Parliament which led to the purchase by Irish tenants of some 220,000 holdings. M.J. O'Connor was a close friend of fellow Wexford man John Edward Redmond, leader of the Irish Parliamentary Party.

Michael O'Connor's brother, James (later Sir James O'Connor), was appointed Solicitor General for Ireland (1914-1917) and then Attorney General. He resigned on the issue of conscription. He was later appointed Privy Counsellor and then Judge of the Chancery Division of the High Court and became Lord Justice of Appeal in 1924. He was also author of two books of law as well as *The History of Ireland 1798-1924*. He took part in peace moves which later led to the Treaty debates. *(Image from the O'Connor collection courtesy of James and Sylvia O'Connor)*

THE O'CONNOR FAMILY connection has continued in the legal practice and is now in its fourth generation. In 2004 M.J. O'Connor and Company moved to larger premises on the outskirts of Wexford. In 2006 the premises was substantially renovated by Greenacres, run by James G. O'Connor and his wife Paula. The building retains many of its finest architectural features. It now incorporates an art gallery, food and wine business and a bistro. The art gallery is one of the finest cultural spaces in Wexford town.

NORTH MAIN STREET

THIS PHOTOGRAPH, WHICH leads us from the Bullring into North Main Street, displays some Flemish gabled houses. Originally built in the early 1700s, the Flemish skylines were added in 1898 as part of a restoration of these houses. They were demolished in the early 1920s. The shop owned by P. Byrne, hardware and coal merchants, to the right of the gabled houses was the home of the rector of St Iberius, Archdeacon John Elgee. His granddaughter Jane, who found fame as the poet Speranza, was widely known for her fiery anti-English prose and verse. She married the Dublin eye and ear surgeon, Dr William Wilde

and was mother of the poet and dramatist Oscar Wilde.

The shop on the corner was owned by John Daly and Son. Further down the street, on the right-hand side was W. and G. Hadden's, founded in 1848. It was a Wexford institution and only ceased business in 1976 when it was taken over by Shaws.

The old Wexford tavern, 'The Cape of Good Hope', is still in existence but has been abridged to 'The Cape'. The apartment above the Cape was the location of the highly publicised murder of Mary Anne Wildes by Simon Bloom on 10 May 1910. Bloom, an artist of Russian origin, served a number of years for the crime and on release emigrated to America. *(Image from the Lawrence collection courtesy of the National Library of Ireland)*

THE NARROWNESS OF the street and the scale of the buildings remain the same. The imitation Flemish style frontage on the building occupied by Boots is still visible.

PAUL
QUAY

THIS SOMEWHAT POSED photograph, with a
row of young boys facing the camera and some
small girls at the gaslight to the right, dates from
about 1900. The ships are topsail schooners. One
of the railway lines heads south to Rosslare with
the town's south station, opened in 1885, just
slightly out of view.

   In the 1830s, a large area of land was reclaimed
from the harbour by the businessman John
Edward Redmond (1806-1865). This extended
south from Paul Quay and led to the creation of
Trinity Street, part of William Street and what is
now Parnell Street. A dockyard was constructed
and it was a major source of employment and
supplied businesses with maritime products such
as sail, rope etc. A large car park in King Street is
still known as the Ropewalk Yard.

What is now the Stonebridge apartment complex was the premises of J.J. Stafford's coal yard and offices. The property extended from Henrietta Street to the corner of King Street. The Staffords were a major business family, being ship owners, importers and exporters. All along Paul Quay cargoes of coal, timber and other commodities were delivered and unloaded. They were the last sail ship owners in Wexford town and in the early 1900s they moved into steamships. During the Second World War they operated the most modern steamship fleet in Ireland, known as the Wexford Steamship Company. A silting of Wexford Harbour and the closure of the port to commercial traffic in the 1950s resulted in Staffords moving most of their business to New Ross. *(Image from the Hayes collection courtesy of John Hayes)*

THERE HAS BEEN major building development on the quay front in recent years. The Stonebridge apartment and retail complex in the right foreground of the picture was built in 2001. The earlier Pierce Court apartment complex is beside it. There is a large six-storey apartment complex known as Seascape Apartments opposite the Talbot Hotel. Wexford Tourist Office is the stone and glass building on the quay front.

PIERCE'S OF WEXFORD

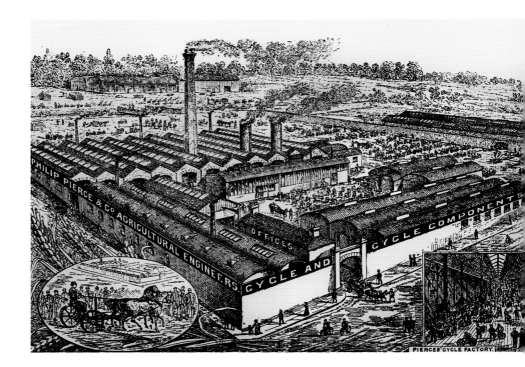

PIERCE'S WAS FOUNDED by James Pierce from Kilmore village in south County Wexford. He was a talented blacksmith, craftsman and inventor who had started making fire fans (or fire machines) in his first Wexford premises in Allen Street in 1839. He then successfully produced horse-powered threshing machines which were a major commercial success. In 1847, he moved to a large 20-acre site at the junction of Mill Road and Distillery Road and the new factory became known as the Folly Mill Road Ironworks.

While his main products were agricultural machinery and implements, he also built the second Wexford bridge at Carcur (1856) and manufactured the elaborate railings for the Twin Churches (1858). Philip Pierce, a son of the founder, succeeded to the business in 1868. With the help of his brother Martin, the business prospered. By 1900 the factory employed 400 workers and the business was the principal industrial employer in the county. Agricultural machinery was exported worldwide.

In 1911 Pierce's and two other machinery manufacturers in the town were at the centre of an industrial dispute of national importance which became known at the Lockout. The issue was the right of ordinary Wexford workers to organise and become members of a trade union. Negotiations were unsuccessful and a protracted and bitter dispute lasted for five months until it was finally resolved in February 1912.

The durability of the farm machinery manufactured by Pierce's militated against repeat orders. As late as 1939 the range of products produced by Pierce's was firmly rooted in the 'horse era' and there was an unwillingness to adapt and change to cater for new markets. It was the end of an era when the company was sold by Philip Pierce in 1964. The legacy of such a major industry and the experience of the Lockout on the whole community in 1911 left an indelible mark on the town. *(Image courtesy of The Irish Agricultural Museum, Johnstown Castle, Wexford)*

TESCO SHOPPING CENTRE has replaced what was once Pierce's, the largest factory in County Wexford. Inside the building can be seen the original clock which used to stand at the factory entrance. Outside, there is a fine sculpture by renowned artist John Atkin. It symbolises the manufacturing carried out by the workers in Pierce's for five generations.

REDMOND SQUARE

THE MONUMENT IN Redmond Square is a tribute to John Edward Redmond, a member of a famous Wexford family. The Redmonds were of Norman descent and towards the end of the 1700s the family became involved in trade, commerce and shipping. John Edward was a liberal MP for the town from 1859 to 1865. It was due to his influence that the railway was brought to Wexford and he was also responsible for the reclamation of 5,000 acres of Wexford harbour, now called the slob lands. His grand-nephew, also called John Edward Redmond (1856-1918), was the leader of the Irish Parliamentary Party after 1900, having reunited the party after the Parnell split. He skilfully secured the passage of the Home Rule Bill through Westminster. The outbreak of the First World War in August 1914 unfortunately delayed the introduction of Home Rule and support for Redmond declined rapidly under pressure of events at home and abroad in the following years. After a lifetime of service to his county and country he died in March 1918 and was buried in the family mausoleum in St John's graveyard.

John's younger brother, William, was killed at the Battle of Messines, south of Ypres in 1917. Willie had been an ardent nationalist member of parliament for thirty-four years. He is buried in Locre in Belgium and Redmond Park on Spawell Road was opened in 1931 in his honour. *(Image from the Lawrence collection courtesy of the National Library of Ireland)*

THE RAILWAY CAME to Wexford in 1872 and the present O'Hanrahan railway station at Redmond Square dates from 1891. Major rebuilding of Redmond Square took place in 1991 as part of an urban renewal project. With some major retail businesses situated here it has given a commercial boost to the north end of Wexford town.

ST IBERIUS' CHURCH

ST IBERIUS' CHURCH is named after St Ibar. Ibar was the first missionary to bring Christianity to Wexford. In the fifth century he established a monastery on Beg Erin (Little Ireland) which is now part of the North Slob, an area of reclaimed land in Wexford harbour. The monastery existed until AD 1160. St Iberius parish was part of the Norse town and was one of five churches within the medieval town walls. It is thought that St Ibar built an oratory on the site of the present church, thus making it one of the oldest centres of Christian worship within the town walls.

The present church was built around 1660. It was enlarged in 1694 and the gallery was built in 1728. In 1760 the architect John Roberts (1712-1796) was commissioned to redesign the church. Due to the narrowness of the site it had to be built on a north-south axis. Roberts was the architect of the Church of Ireland and Catholic cathedrals in Waterford city and built in a Georgian style. While St Iberius is aesthetically pleasing on the street front, its shape and internal decor are surprising. There is a striking arcaded chancel screen and ornate stucco plasterwork at the top of the two Corinthian columns. The belfry was a nineteenth-century addition. The church boasts an impressive number of substantial wall-mounted funeral monuments.

The rector of St Iberius 1795-1823 was Archdeacon John Elgee. He is said to have accompanied many of his congregation to their execution on Wexford bridge during the 1798 rebellion. Members of the Church of Ireland community fought on the loyalist and rebel sides in the rebellion. John Elgee's daughter, Jane, was the mother of Arctic explorer

Robert McClure who was born in Wexford in 1807. The last of the Elgee family, Edith, died in Wexford in 1993. Refurbishment of the church took place in the early 1990s. Major structural work was undertaken and the interior was restored to its former glory. *(Image from the Lawrence collection courtesy of the National Library of Ireland)*

THE CHURCH IS open to the public every day and is primarily a place of worship. However, it is also a venue for concerts, recitals and other events throughout the year. Today, it is very much a focal point for the whole community in the heart of Wexford.

ST JOHN OF
GOD CONVENT

THIS PHOTOGRAPH IS of the St John of God convent on Newtown road which was built in 1881. It was founded a decade earlier through the initiative of seven sisters of the Bon Secours community in Paris and Bishop Thomas Furlong (1803-1875) of the Diocese of Ferns. In post-Famine Ireland people were still suffering great poverty, hunger and disease. Some of the nuns were experienced nurses and nursed the sick in their own homes. In 1872 two nuns went to work in the infirmary in Wexford Union Workhouse which was later to house Wexford General Hospital. They also worked in fever hospitals in response to outbreaks of typhoid fever in a number of dioceses.

The sisters were involved in education as well as health care, believing in the value of education as a means towards alleviation of poverty. They taught first in the schoolroom in Wexford Union Workhouse. They took over a school in the Faythe in 1875. Later their involvement in education expanded to schools in several dioceses in Ireland, England, Wales and Western Australia.

A mission was established to Australia in 1895. The sisters continue their ministry there to this present day. The number of young women joining the congregation both in Ireland and Australia, continued to grow and within a few decades of the foundation, the ministry of the Sisters of St John of God extended to many parts of Ireland, England, Nigeria, Pakistan, Cameroon, Australia and most recently South Africa through their education and healthcare facilities. *(Image courtesy of An tAthair Séamus S de Vál)*

FROM ITS FOUNDATION in Wexford in 1871, the St John of God sisters have ministered worldwide but, with a decline in personnel in the 1970s and 1980s, the congregation had to reassess their role.

In Wexford the sisters continue to be involved in many and varied ministries. The convent is now a retirement home for twenty-nine sisters. In the convent grounds is Sallyville House, the original convent, and now the Congregation's Heritage Centre which opened in 2007.

ST PETER'S COLLEGE

THE IMPOSING FAÇADE of St Peter's College, on its elevated
site, dominates the skyline as one enters the town over Wexford
bridge. A Roman Catholic Seminary had existed in Bunker's Hill
(Michael Street) since 1811 and the staff and students transferred
to their new home in St Peter's College in 1819. The site, with a fine
three-storey dwelling in the right-hand side of the photograph dates
from the 1790s. The impressive east façade was designed by Wexford
architect and builder Richard Pierce and was completed between
1829 and 1832. He was the architect of Wexford's Twin Churches.
An elegant tower in the centre of a castellated frontage backs onto
a quadrangle of school buildings.

From its foundation the college has catered for both boarders
and day pupils and for students intended for the priesthood. Priests
ordained in St Peter's have ministered throughout the world.
The college has expanded with a number of major additions over
the years. In 1878-79 St Aidan's, a large building behind the college
chapel which included a study hall with dormitories, was constructed.
As the number of ecclesiastical students increased it was necessary to
build a completely new wing incorporating a concert hall in 1938.

The capacity of the secondary school was greatly enhanced in
1969-70 with the opening of St Ibar's wing which completed the
western side of the college quadrangle. Due to decreasing residential
student numbers it was decided to close the boarding school in 1997
and the seminary in 1998. The college has a long and proud Gaelic

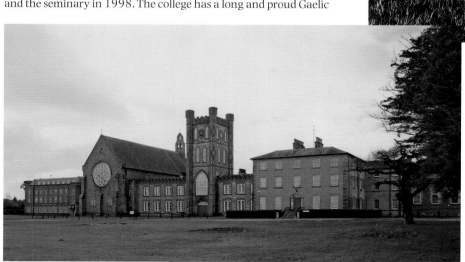

Athletic Association tradition with a number of All-Ireland titles. It also has a strong musical and theatrical tradition. The college has produced many important figures in Church and State. Among its former students are historian and Primate of All Ireland, Cardinal Tomas Ó Fiaich (1923-1990); the current provost of Trinity College Dublin, Dr Patrick Prendergast; and the distinguished writers John Banville and Colm Tóibín. *(Image from the Lawrence collection courtesy of the National Library of Ireland)*

ST PETER'S COLLEGE today has a fine reputation as a secondary school with over 700 students. Recent extensions and refurbishments have greatly enhanced educational facilities at the school. With the closure of the seminary in 1998 the Wexford Campus of the Institute of Technology, Carlow took over the building and it now has an enrolment of 900 students.

ST PETER'S COLLEGE CHAPEL

THE COLLEGE CHAPEL, designed by Augustus Welby Pugin, contains many of the features that distinguish his unique architectural style such as a rood screen seen to the forefront of the picture, separating the nave and the choir, and the beautifully painted altar triptych. Pugin (1812-1852), a convert to Catholicism, is considered to be one of the finest exponents of Gothic Revival architecture. He is remembered today as one of the designers of the Palace of Westminster – his most iconic contribution to that project is the clock tower which houses Big Ben. Pugin came to prominence in England mainly through the patronage of John Talbot, 16th Earl of Shrewsbury. Talbot had close family ties with influential Irish Catholic families which resulted in several commissions to build and design churches in the Diocese of Ferns.

The college chapel is unique in that it shows his ideas on church architecture early in his career. The foundation stone for the church was laid by Bishop James Keating on 18 June 1838 and Pugin attended, reputedly in full medieval dress. He only visited St Peter's on

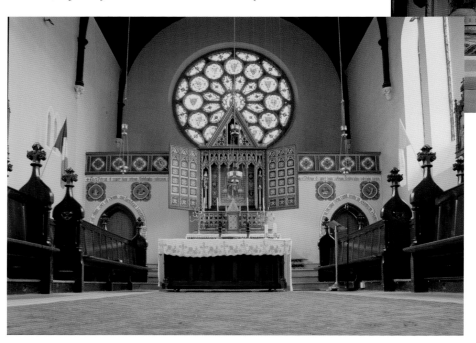

two or three more occasions and most of the work was left to local builders. The chapel was completed in 1840. The large rose window tracery was actually completed in wood; the grey paint work makes it appear like stone. The stained glass is attributed to John Hardman. The patrons, the Talbot family, are remembered by their coat of arms surrounding the central glass pane. There is a strong Marian theme in the woodcarving and paintings in the altar. *(Image from the Lawrence collection courtesy of the National Library of Ireland)*

THE MAIN FABRIC of the Chapel is still intact as is the main altar. The rood screen that separated the nave and the choir was regrettably removed in 1950 and the seating was set out in collegiate style where members of the congregation face each other across the aisle. The chapel is still used for liturgies and for other college ceremonies.

SELSKAR ABBEY

THIS PHOTOGRAPH DISPLAYS the shell of a former Church of Ireland church built in 1826 and decommissioned in 1956. The complex of buildings on this site is of particular interest as it shows one of the earliest ecclesiastical sites in the town which is still with us after more than 800 years. The fortified tower, possibly added in the fourteenth century, is well preserved and was completely restored in the early nineteenth century. Directly behind the early nineteenth-century church are the thirteenth-century ruins of the priory of SS Peter and Paul, better known as Selskar Abbey.

The abbey was founded early in the thirteenth century by the Canon Regulars of St Augustine. Some historians have claimed that there may have been an earlier

pre-Norman church located here due to the topography of the site. Wexford is a complex of medieval parishes some being within the town wall, such as Selskar, and others outside.

The town wall divided the monastic site with Westgate Tower as we know it today providing access between both areas. Nothing remains of the monastic buildings. The tower and part of the church survive inside the walls. Selskar Priory had a double nave separated by an arcade of four arches which is largely destroyed except for the gables. There are remnants of west windows and an arcade of four pointed arches separating the aisles.

The foundation of Selskar has been attributed to the Roche family but it is more likely to have been the Marshall family. Dissolution came in the 1540s and the abbey was retained as a Protestant place of worship. This meant that Selskar did not experience the same fate as other medieval churches in the town which were dismantled and their stone used in other buildings. It was, however, destroyed by Cromwellian soldiers in 1649. *(Image from the Lawrence collection courtesy of the National Library of Ireland)*

THE BUILDING OF the new church, designed by John Semple, on the ancient site in 1826 was controversial as it involved demolishing part of the old abbey to make way for the new church. The fourteenth-century tower was restored and used as a sacristy and belfry. Recently the site has been revamped by Wexford Lions Club in co-operation with Wexford Borough Council. There are regular tours of the abbey. It is well worth a visit.

SELSKAR AVENUE

TRIMMER'S LANE IS known today as Selskar Avenue. The historian Nicky Rossiter has written a detailed article in the *Journal of the Wexford Historical Society*, No.19, on the history of laneways in Wexford town. He points out that prior to 1847 most streets did not have official names. Trimmer was a name given to sailors who trimmed or distributed ballast to give an unladen ship better balance. The street photographed here was Trimmer's Lane West, which runs from Selskar Abbey and crosses Selskar Street where it becomes Trimmer's Lane East ending at the Quay. It is first mentioned in 1583

and was an important route from Selskar Abbey to the ferry point on the Quay. In 1919 a row of dilapidated houses was demolished in Trimmer's Lane and the resulting open area was renamed Selskar Avenue. The photograph depicts the area in the late 1950s or early '60s in a poor state of repair. *(Image from the John Scanlon collection courtesy of Dominic Kiernan)*

THE BUILDING ON the right-hand side of the street is Greenacres (see pp. 34-35). To the left of the modern photograph is a statue of the Wexford hurling legend Nickey Rackard (1922-1976). He is widely regarded as one of the greatest hurlers of all-time. He won two All-Ireland titles in 1955 and 1956. He was a member of the Wexford senior team from 1940 until 1956. Wexford Borough Council commissioned leading British portrait sculptor Mark Richards to cast the statue of Rackard in his hurling prime and it was unveiled in 2012.

In the 1990s an urban renewal project in this area Abbey resulted in a number of new businesses and restaurants opening and new life has been injected into the surrounding streets.

SHIPS ON THE QUAY

THIS PHOTOGRAPH, WHICH dates from about 1900, shows a long line of topsail schooners on Wexford Quays. Wexford Harbour has been a trading port from earliest times. Wexford, or Waes Fjord as Wexford was known then (meaning the 'inlet of the mud flats'), was given this name by the Vikings. With the arrival of the Normans in 1169 the port was to become a major exporting port and by the fifteenth and sixteenth centuries it was a major fishing port exporting to ports across the Irish Sea.

By the mid-1640s, Wexford Harbour had become a base for privateering ships owned by the Irish, French and Flemish. In the late 1640s, there were over 400 ships operating out of Wexford, attacking English ships. Wexford was a geographically strategic location and the harbour was a safe base due to its shallowness which prevented attacking ships entering it. Oliver Cromwell arrived in Wexford in 1649 and retribution was meted out to its inhabitants.

In the late eighteenth century Wexford's chief exports were corn, herrings, beer, beef, hides, tallow and butter. Goods were exported worldwide and luxury goods were imported. The town continued to prosper and by 1788 it was the sixth busiest port in Ireland.

In 1846 a major project was undertaken to reclaim 3,000 hectares of land from the harbour, known today as the North and South Slob. This reduced the area of the harbour by 50 per cent. Tidal flows changed and major silting resulted. Despite various remedial works by the Harbour Commissioners the silting of the harbour continued. By the late 1950s the port was no longer viable and it closed to commercial traffic in 1968. The port had been extremely important to the local economy and its closure led to a downturn in the Wexford economy. In the early 1900s a new port was built at Rosslare Harbour which is used by the main ferry companies to France and Wales. *(Image from the Lawrence collection courtesy of the National Library of Ireland)*

THE PORT IS now used exclusively by mussel dredgers and pleasure craft. The woodenworks which fronted the quays and were synonymous with the port were removed in the 1990s to create a new pedestrianised amenity area for the town.

SOUTH MAIN STREET

THIS PHOTOGRAPH REVEALS a busy South
Main Street, Wexford's main shopping street, around
1900. The hardware business in the right-hand side
of the photograph was owned by John Sinnott, twice
Mayor of Wexford, owner of two ironmongery stores
and a general hardware shop, as well as the Theatre
Royal. It was originally Kenny's Hall or Castle.

In the 1400s there were at least six tower houses
built within the walls of the town. One of these
was a square turreted tower known as Kenny's Hall
and the base of the castle was visible until recent
years. One side of the basement ran along Kayser's
lane, a laneways dating from the Viking period. It is
commonly accepted that Oliver Cromwell stayed
there during the winter of 1649. It was also the
headquarters of Colonel David Sinnott, governor of the
town prior to its capture by Cromwell.

The early seventeenth century was a tumultuous
period for the inhabitants of the town as political
and religious conflict erupted. In 1641 the former
landowners who had been dispossessed rebelled and

conflict between Catholic and Protestant townspeople arose. The harbour became a base for the forces of the Federation of Kilkenny. In October 1649 Oliver Cromwell arrived in Wexford with a cavalry of 7,000 to seek revenge on the Catholics of Wexford. He captured the Fort of Rosslare, landed his artillery and, with the town surrounded, negotiations began; but before they were concluded, Cromwell's forces entered the town and ran amok.

According to Cromwell's later report to Parliament almost 2,000 inhabitants perished. There is no accurate record. All that is known is that Wexford and its inhabitants were devastated and it took the town a long time to recover. *(Image from the Lawrence collection courtesy of the National Library of Ireland)*

TODAY THE SITE of the castle is occupied by Penny's department store. From 1952 until 1984 it housed FW Woolworth and Company, part of an American chain of shops. A brass plaque on the outside of the building reminds us of the building's historical significance.

THE BULLRING

THE BULLRING GOT its name from the medieval sport of bull baiting. It was introduced in 1621 by the town's Butchers' Guild. Baiting took place each year in August and November, with the hide of the beast being presented to the mayor and the meat being given to feed the poor. The practice ended in 1770. Furlong's butchers, which trades in the Bullring today, was established 1621. Despite popular belief there is little historical evidence that a massacre took place in the Bullring during the assault on the town by Cromwell's forces in 1649.

During the 1798 rebellion, the Bullring became an open-air armaments factory, making and repairing pikes and other weapons for the insurgents. Ireland's first declaration as a republic was made here in 1798. Lord Kingsborough, one of the government commanders during the 1798 rebellion, was held captive in the building in

the left foreground of the photograph, known today as 'The Cape'. The statue of The Pikeman, erected in 1905, has huge symbolic significance for Wexford and was designed by the distinguished sculptor Oliver Sheppard. It dominates the Bullring. Sheppard was also responsible for many of the 1798 memorials in County Wexford.

In the right-hand side of the photograph is The Tholsel, which was built in 1794 and was the Mayor's Court or Town Hall. It housed the Corporation and Mayor's Court of Conscience 1805-1890. It was demolished in 1898. The Market House in the centre of the photograph dates from 1871.

There is a plaque close to the present-day Furlong's butchers erected in 1961 to honour a famous Wexford boxer, Jem Roche. During his sporting life of thirty-eight fights, he won twenty-two by knockout and seven on points. He lost the World Heavyweight boxing championship in Dublin to T. Burns on 17 March 1908. *(Image from the Eason collection courtesy of the National Library of Ireland)*

THE BULLRING WAS completely refurbished as part of the bicentenary celebrations of 1998 when the statue of the Pikeman was repositioned. A 'Tree of Liberty', an oak, has been planted in the centre of the square and limestone slabs feature inscriptions relating to 1798. Bollards in the shape of canons line the area. The new-look square was officially opened by President Mary McAleese in May 1998. The recently refurbished Market House has brought business back into the Bullring.

THE FAYTHE

THE FAYTHE COMES from the word *faiche*, meaning fair green.
In the past, when fairs were only held twice a year, the location
alternated between John Street and the Faythe. This was a
close-knit community and the distinctive characteristic of this
suburb is its long affinity with the sea. Generations of sailors
have come from here and have worked throughout the world.

In the top right-hand corner of the photograph, slightly out
of view, is the graveyard of St Michael. It is the site of one of
the earliest churches in Wexford. The church was destroyed
by Cromwellian forces and its stones used to repair Wexford
Castle which stood nearby. The castle was a fortified military
post for over 1,000 years and played a vital role during the
Cromwellian siege of 1649.

The houses in Swan View date from the mid-nineteenth
century. In the top right of the photograph is a malt house and
one on the other side of the street. Both are now converted
into apartments. In 1806, there were as many as thirty-three
licenced malt houses in the town. The production of whiskey
was vital to the local economy.

During the 1911 Lockout, the labour leader James Larkin
addressed the foundry workers in this area. *(Image from the
Lawrence collection courtesy of the National Library of Ireland)*

IN THE CURRENT photograph there are three interesting monuments, one old and two recent ones. The Swan, which gives the area its name, is a fountain which was donated by Mrs Elizabeth 'Lady Dane' Deane Morgan of Ardcandrisk House on behalf of the County Wexford Society for the Prevention of Cruelty to Animals. There is a new monument to all Wexford men lost in past wars. The Lockout Gate was unveiled by President Michael D. Higgins in May 2012. A literary association with this location is that the internationally renowned author John Banville was born in the Faythe in 1945. He is the author of twenty-three novels, including *The Sea*, which won the 2005 Man Booker prize.

THE FRIARY

THE FRANCISCANS ARRIVED in Wexford around 1255. A small
chapel and a cemetery originally set aside for the Knights
Hospitallers of St John were given to the Friars by Maurice Fitzgerald
as their new foundation, which was situated outside the town wall
at Kaysers gate. Eight hundred years later, despite the often very
turbulent political and religious history of Wexford, the Franciscans
occupy the same site today.

The friary was confiscated in 1540 and the friars were expelled.
By 1560 the church was in ruins and its stones were used to repair
Wexford Castle. In 1620 the friars rented a house in High Street and
built a thatched chapel in Archer's Lane on the site of the present
Opera House. Oliver Cromwell arrived in Wexford in October 1649
and among his victims were members of the Franciscan community.
By 1690, however, the Franciscan community had rebuilt their
church and this building served as the parish church of Wexford
until the Twin Churches were opened in 1858.

By 1780 the church had to be enlarged and the following year,
under the direction of Fr John Corrin the church was enhanced
by Doric style windows and interior columns. As congregations
increased, the transept north of the east gable was added in 1812

followed by internal galleries in 1827. The handsome Romanesque bell-tower was built in 1856. Its campanile is still dominant on the Wexford skyline. The substantial building on the right-hand side of the photograph is the residence of the Franciscan community.

The interior of the Friary has a fine ornate barrel ceiling separated from the side isles by a colonnade of eight massive pillars which support a beautiful panelled ceiling. This work was completed by the Wexford builder Patrick O'Connor in 1861-62. *(Image from the Lawrence collection courtesy of the National Library of Ireland)*

IN 1984, EXTENSIVE dry rot was discovered in the fabric of the church. A major fundraising drive took place and the building was extensively renovated. During the building work the Franciscans were allowed to use St Iberius' church by the Church of Ireland community. The church re-opened in 1987. In 2007, the Friars Minor (Brown Friars) left Wexford and the Conventual (Grey Friars) continue the Franciscan presence in the town.

THE QUAYS
FROM THE
BALLAST BANK

THE BOAT IN the foreground of this photograph is moored at the Ballast Bank. It was built in 1831 to allow boats leaving the quays without cargo to take on ballast of rocks or sand for stability. Ships arriving with ballast could deposit it on the island and then take on their new cargo.

The Crescent was once the deep Pool of Wexford around which the Viking town was built. Estuaries of streams converged here and created an anchorage point. When the quays were built in the early 1800s the flow of water was altered and the Crescent silted up. A railway bridge was built across the Crescent in 1882. The large warehouse to the right of the Harbour Board offices was used to store whiskey from Bishopswater Distillery prior to export and a number of malt stores are visible at the Crescent.

Also visible are large quantities of timber. Much of this would have been of Canadian origin, shipped across the Atlantic to be processed at the saw mills of the Crescent. The large building on the Crescent is the Harbour Commissioners Office and Ballast Office, built in 1838. This would have been a very important building in the heyday of Wexford Port. The substantial building at

the corner of the Crescent housed the Bank of Ireland and was built in 1835. It was one of the earliest purpose-built banks in the locality. The importance attached to the port by the banks is obvious because there are two other financial institutions close by. Further along the quay at the corner of Anne Street and Common Quay is a fine Victorian building which was the Provincial Bank and is now Wexford Credit Union. The most ornate building in this area is the old National Bank with sculptured figureheads. It is now the studios of South East radio. *(Image from the Lawrence collection courtesy of the National Library of Ireland)*

TODAY THE QUAYS are very different. The development of the quay front and the provision of a marina at the Crescent created a new amenity area for the people of Wexford. There have been many commercial and residential developments along the quays in recent years in response to this development.

RAILWAY

THE FACT THAT the railway line runs along the quay front alongside road traffic, and that until 1977 Wexford had two railway stations, makes the railway line through the town somewhat unique.

A rail link between Dublin and Wexford was first proposed in 1844 by the famed engineer of the Great Western Railway (GWR), Isambard Kingdom Brunel. GWR opened a railway line to Wicklow in 1855; the line was then extended to Enniscorthy in 1864 and reached Wexford in 1872. The extension into County Wexford saw the title of the company altered to the Dublin, Wicklow & Wexford Railway.

In 1869, an application was lodged by the Wexford and Waterford Railway to Wexford Harbour Board Commissioners to run a tramway along the quays to connect the two railways. This was granted but the company was required to build a wooden quay front to facilitate a second line of rails to act as a siding for the loading and unloading of shipping vessels alongside. Hence the 'woodenworks' came into being. The construction of a bridge over the Crescent commenced in 1880 and the rail link to Rosslare opened in 1882.

A temporary station had been opened in August 1872 at Carcur, beside the present-day boat club, an extension to the present station being opened in 1879. The current station building dates from 1891. A second station was opened by the Waterford & Wexford Railway

in William Street in 1885 and was named South Wexford, later Wexford South. The woodenworks provided rail access to ships unloading their cargo and was in commercial use until the 1950s. *(Image courtesy of* The Irish Times*)*

THE WOODENWORKS FELL into disrepair with the decline of shipping and lack of maintenance by CIE and as part of a main drainage scheme they were removed in the 1990s.

The area was in filled and a new quay front of 25 metres depth built. Part of the quay front was paved with wooden decking to resemble the old quay front and the bollards where ships had been tied up were reinstated. A major new amenity area was provided for the town.

The railway still runs along the quay front and Irish Rail currently operates five services between Rosslare and Dublin each day. Running along the Slaney and Wicklow coastline, it is one of the most scenic railway journeys in the country.

THEATRE ROYAL

BEHIND THIS ROW of houses and its unimposing entrance lay the Theatre Royal. It hosted opera, light opera, drama, pantomime and other performances down through the years and was a cinema for a time. It served the people of Wexford and beyond for 174 years, until its demolition in 2006 to make way for the new Opera House. The theatre was built by William Taylor, printer and publisher of a local newspaper, the *Wexford Herald*. It opened to the public in January 1832. Prior to 1830 Wexford had a regular playhouse in Cornmarket as well as one in Church Lane and a third theatre is said to have existed in the eighteenth century on Spawell Road. *(Image from the Denis O'Connor collection courtesy of Denise O'Connor Murphy)*

THERE IS A long musical tradition in Wexford both in opera and in more popular music. Throughout the nineteenth century the Theatre Royal attracted leading singers from Opera Houses in London. The famous author and lecturer Hilaire Belloc spoke in the Theatre on 1 November 1910. Local drama and musical performances took place and, from the early 1900s, Wexford's Amateur Light Opera Society (the forerunner of Wexford Light Opera Society) produced many shows. The first film was screened in 1902 and within a

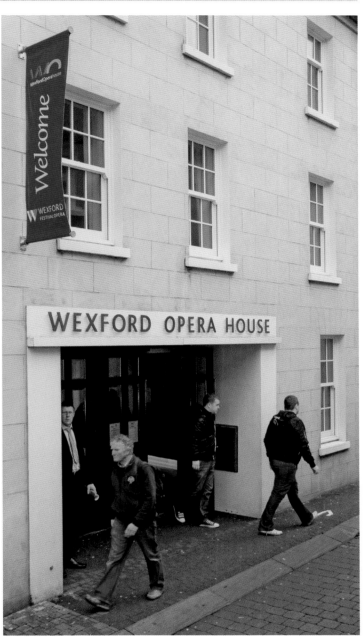

decade films were screened on a weekly basis. In 1942, the building underwent its first major reconstruction. Local musical and drama groups were to be the principal users of the Theatre and quality productions attracted full houses. Touring companies which included Lord Longford, Micheál MacLiammóir and Hilton Edwards also performed in The Theatre.

WEXFORD FESTIVAL OPERA AND OPERA HOUSE

WEXFORD FESTIVAL OPERA began when the Scottish novelist and music critic Sir Compton McKenzie suggested in a talk to Wexford Opera Study Circle in 1950 that they should stage their own opera. The Theatre Royal was acquired in the same year by Wexford Festival Council. Dr Tom Walsh, the main driving force behind the opera festival, and a group of fellow opera lovers staged the first opera, *The Rose of Castile*, in 1951. Dr Tom Walsh served as artistic director for sixteen years and his leadership and inspiration through difficult economic times meant that the festival survived and prospered. He was recognised internationally as an expert on opera having published several books on the subject. Wexford has always attracted rising young opera singers and has staged less well-known operas. This continued to be a winning formula down through the years.

The festival has grown from strength to strength and attracts internationally renowned artists and cosmopolitan audiences every autumn. International critics have lauded Wexford for its unique operatic experience. Another unique aspect of the festival is the huge voluntary input by the people of Wexford to the running of the festival. A brave decision was taken in 1995 to build a new opera house. It took thirteen years and €33 million from inception to completion and it was opened to the public in the autumn of 2008. *(Image courtesy of Pádraig Grant)*

WEXFORD OPERA HOUSE is Ireland's first custom-built, multipurpose opera house.
The complex seats 780 people in its main auditorium and 175 in its smaller theatre. The main
auditorium is walnut lined with blue leather seating and features horseshoe-shaped balconies.
The design brings audiences and performers in close proximity to each other. The size of the
original entrance and the streetscape has been retained but the interior of the Opera House
surprises all those who have not visited it before. It is a secret gem in the heart of Wexford. It is
a huge credit to the individuals who worked so hard to make the dream become a reality. It will
continue to be at the centre of cultural life in Wexford and Ireland for years to come.

THOMAS MOORE TAVERN

A PUBLIC HOUSE has existed on this site since about 1750. 'Molly Mythen's' bar, seen in the centre of the photograph, is on the site of the original building. Thomas Moore's grandfather lived there and his mother, Anastasia Codd, was born there. Moore was born on 28 May 1779 in Aungier Street, Dublin. While attending Trinity College, Dublin, he became friendly with Robert Emmet and was influenced by his political views. He also associated with members of the United Irishmen. His political views from this period influenced his later poetic and literary works. He did not take part in the 1798 rebellion. The following year he moved to London.

He became a close friend of Lord Byron and in 1817 published *Lalla Rookh*, a long oriental poem, which was an instant success. In the English-speaking world only Lord

Byron and Sir Walter Scott rivalled Moore for popular and critical acclaim. He wrote biographies of the playwright Richard Brindsley Sheridan, the United Irish leader Lord Edward Fitzgerald and the poet Lord Byron.

He is best known for his ten volumes of Irish melodies, based on his poetry and published between 1803 and 1834, which were hugely successful throughout the world. The combination of Irish airs and the poetry of Moore's lyrics transcended class and nationalities. He was acclaimed as Ireland's national poet.

Thomas Moore visited his mother's birthplace on 26 August 1835. He later visited the Presentation Convent in Francis Street where he planted a myrtle tree and played the organ in the convent chapel. His family connection with Wexford is marked by a plaque on the first floor of the Thomas Moore Tavern. The present plaque was erected in 1926 by the Uí Cinsealaigh Historical Society replacing the original which was damaged by weathering. *(Image courtesy of Wexford County Council Library Services)*

THE CURRENT PROPERTY has undergone major refurbishment in recent years by the Wright family who own and run the business.

THE TOWN WALL

WHEN THE ANGLO Normans arrived in Wexford there were already town defences in existence since Viking times. Ramparts had been built and possibly some stone walls. Not only were the walls for defensive purposes but they also fulfilled a political and economic function and were a line of demarcation between the burgesses of the town and outsiders.

The medieval town enclosed by the town wall was long and narrow. The building of the wall commenced in the early 1200s and it is estimated it took approximately fifty years to complete. The walls were three-quarters of a mile long and encompassed approximately forty statute acres. The southern stretch of Norman wall followed the line of the Viking wall but how far north it went is unknown. A castle was built in the south of the town and there were seven town gates. The walls curved down to the sea close to Westgate in the north and Wexford Castle in the south end of town.

The only surviving gate, now called Westgate and fully restored in the 1980s, was not a public town gate but rather an entrance to Selskar Abbey. The historian George Griffiths claims that many of the town gates were removed by the Corporation in 1759. They were re-erected after the 1798 rebellion and removed again in 1835. The fabric of the walls varies from section to section.

This photograph shows the outside of the town wall between George's Street and Selskar Gate (later known as Westgate). It served as a gate for the abbey which had property on both sides of the wall. This is one of the most visible stretches of the town wall and was probably the last portion of the wall to be constructed. The tower of Selskar Gate is somewhat obscured by a tree and the tower of Selskar Abbey, restored in 1826 at the same time that Selskar church was built. *(Image from the John Scanlon collection courtesy of Dominic Kiernan)*

AS IS OBVIOUS from the modern photograph, much restoration work has been carried out on this section of the wall. Westgate tower was completely restored in the 1980s. The stretch of the wall including the mural tower has been restored and an amenity area for pedestrians has been developed. The town walls are a protected structure and are listed as being of national significance.

THE
TWIN CHURCHES

THE TWO ELEGANT tapering spires of Wexford's
'Twin Churches' have dominated the Wexford skyline for
over 150 years. One can only imagine the effect these two
magnificent structures had in a town like Wexford a few years
after the Great Famine. They were an affirmation of a resurgent
Irish Catholicism of the early nineteenth century.

In 1850, at a public meeting in the Franciscan church, it
was decided due to the increasing demands of the church-going
population to build not one, but two new churches in the town,
one for the south end and one for the north end. There had been
no parochial church in Wexford since 1692, the Franciscan
church having fulfilled this role. The then Bishop of Ferns, Myles
Murphy, stipulated that both churches 'be identical in plan to avoid
jealousy and unpleasant comparisons amongst the townspeople'.
The Church of the Assumption was built at Bride Street on a
vacant plot which contained the site of the medieval graveyard of
St Brigid and a Quaker graveyard. The Church of the Immaculate

Conception was built at Rowe Street and involved the demolition of some houses and part of the old town wall. The churches were sited within 500 metres of each other.

The driving force behind the fundraising was Fr James Roche, who had become parish priest of Wexford in 1850. Funding came from wealthy individuals in Wexford, Irish exiles throughout the world, households in Wexford through a weekly collection known as chapel rent and sailors landing on Wexford quays. Fr Roche died in 1883 and in his honour a statue by Sir Thomas Farrell was erected in the grounds of Rowe Street church. Fr Roche is interred in a tomb in Bride Street church. *(Image from the Lawrence collection courtesy of the National Library of Ireland)*

OVER THE YEARS alterations have been made to both churches. The altar in Bride Street was removed in the 1960s and replaced by a modern marble altar and the original sacristy in Bride Street became the chapel of the Convent of the Perpetual Adoration.

THE TWIN CHURCHES

THE CHURCHES WERE built to a design by Richard Pierce from Tenacre, County Wexford who had acted as Clerk of Works for Augustus Welby Pugin on the building of St Aidan's Cathedral, Enniscorthy as well as Killarney Cathedral and Maynooth College. Pierce did not live to see his Twin Churches completed, dying in 1854. The architect J.J. McCarthy finished his work.

Both churches are built of local sandstone from Park Quarry and granite from Wicklow. Each church is 166ft in length and 60ft in breadth. The towers are 16ft square and the walls are 5ft thick and 105ft in height on four levels. The beautiful tapering spires are 222ft in height. The boundary walls are built of the same stone as the churches and the very ornate railings were manufactured by Pierce's Foundry.

Inside the churches the elaborate altars and reredos were made of Caen stone. The nave is separated from the aisles by colonnades of pointed arches supported by granite pillars. The fine stained-glass windows have the names of the donors placed underneath. The East window in Rowe street depicting a Calvary scene was the gift of James and Anne Behan, the children of James Roche's first teacher, a Protestant. The east window of Bride Street displaying the Ascension is equally fine. Of special note

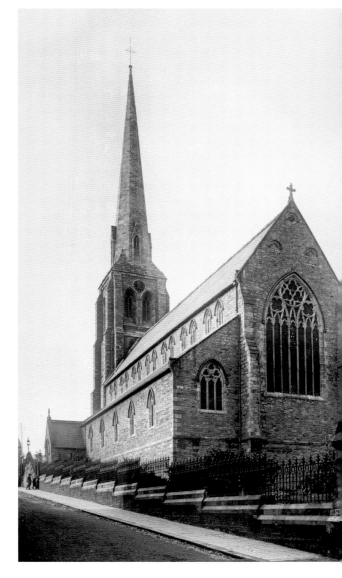

also is the O'Keefe memorial window in Bride Street dating from 1917 designed by Ireland's foremost symbolist artist Harry Clarke. Another unique feature of both churches is the very fine Telford organs. Rowe Street church holds the oldest parish registers in Ireland dating from 1672. *(Image from the Lawrence collection courtesy of the National Library of Ireland)*

MORTUARIES HAVE BEEN added to both churches and the grounds have been reorganised in recent years to make way for public car parks, the proceeds of which help hugely in defraying the maintenance cost of the buildings. Both buildings are an enduring source of pride to the people of Wexford town.

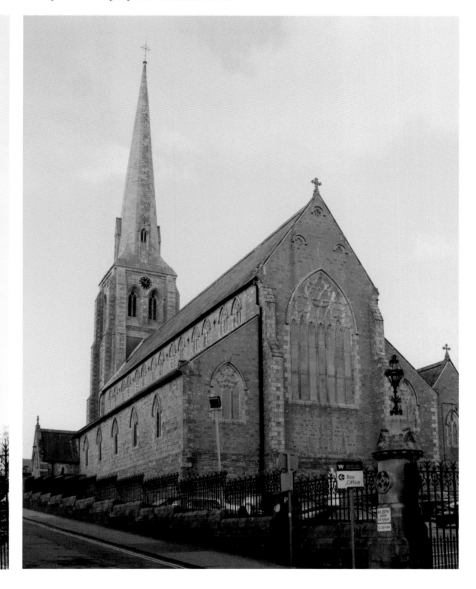

THE VALOTTIN
MONUMENT

WYGRAM PLACE AT the top of Hill Street has been an important road
intersection from earliest times. The Wygram family owned Wygram House,
which still exists close to the monument. Today, this triangular area is known as
Monument Place as the simple stone obelisk seen in the photograph was erected
here in memory of Major Charles Valottin, a veteran of the war in Spain, who
died at this spot in 1793.

Tensions had been rising throughout County Wexford in the years prior to
this event as a result of a campaign for the non-payment of tithes (taxes paid to
the Established Church). Sixteen men had been arrested in Bunclody. Fourteen
were released but two were imprisoned in Wexford jail. A large group of
protestors marched to Wexford to demand their release. They were met by Major
Charles Vallotin and a group of fifty soldiers at Windmill Hill. Valottin came
forward to negotiate with John Moore from Palace, near New Ross, the leader
of the protestors. Valottin noticed one of his officers being held prisoner by the
crowd and thrust his sword into Moore. In response Moore struck his assailant
with a scythe. Both men were mortally wounded. The soldiers opened fire
and many were killed. Others who tried to flee were killed by Captain Boyd in
an ambush at Bettyville. Five others found hiding in a hay barn were tried,
convicted and executed on Windmill Hill. The events of the day caused great fear
throughout the town and county. It has been referred to as 'the First Rebellion'
in County Wexford. 1798 was to follow five years later. In the Corporation
Minute Book it is recorded that on 30 September 1793 it was decided to erect a

monument to Major Charles Valottin of the 69th Infantry who 'fell in defence of the town of Wexford when attacked by a dangerous and riotous mob'. He is also commemorated by a large wall-mounted monument in St Iberius' church. *(Image from the John Scanlon collection courtesy of Dominic Kiernan)*

THE RECESSED BUILDING on the right-hand side, behind the railings, was once one house and served as a Lying-in-Hospital. It is now divided into two houses. The tall building to the right, where Gaynor's grocery shop and public house are today was owned by the Walsh family. Three famous Wexford people grew up here: John (Sandy) Walsh, actor of stage and screen; Dr Tom Walsh author, founder and artistic director of Wexford Festival Opera; and Miss Nellie Walsh, contralto. The large brick building adjacent to Monument Place was, until recently, the offices of Wexford Borough Council and previously Wexford Corporation. It was once the Tate school funded by a bequest from William Tate who had made his fortune in the Jamaica sugar trade. One of its most famous pupils was the short story writer and novelist William Trevor who attended school here in the early 1940s.

WESTGATE TOWER

THE MEDIEVAL TOWN walls dating from the early 1200s were three-quarters of a mile long and encompassed approximately forty statute acres. A castle was built in the south of the town. There were seven town gates from north to south: West (Cow) Gate, Selskar Gate, John's Gate, Friars' Gate, Peter's Gate, Bride Gate and Castle Gate. The structure now known as Westgate Tower was fully restored in the 1980s. However, it was not a public town gate but rather an entrance to Selskar Abbey. The abbey had property on both sides of the wall. With the removal of the original Westgate which was situated on the street, the name Westgate was transferred to Selskar Gate. The actual tower over the present Westgate is probably a fourteenth-century addition and is known as a gate-tower.

Quoting a letter in 1835, the Wexford historian Herbert Francis Hore claimed the walls were completed in 1300 by Sir Stephen Devereux. When the town gates were demolished in the late eighteenth century, to make way for traffic, Westgate was left in place as it was not being used for access the town. The tower is three stories high over a vaulted ground floor gateway. Both the second and third floors each have a fireplace and a garderobe. There is a doorway on the second floor leading to a walkway along the town wall and on the parapet there are lookout platforms. *(Image courtesy of An tAthair Séamus S de Vál)*

WESTGATE TOWER WAS restored by Wexford Borough Council in May, 1990 and was recipient of a Europa Nostra Award for restoration and adaptation of a historic building.

WEXFORD BRIDGES

THE BRIDGE IN this photograph, erected in 1856, linked Carcur to Crosstown. At the top of the photograph one can see St Ibar's cemetery, the main graveyard for Wexford town since 1892. James Pierce of the Mill Road Foundry Iron Works built the new structure at Carcur. He also manufactured the elaborate railings for the Twin Churches (1858). This bridge preceded the present Wexford Bridge spanning the Slaney from Commercial Quay to Ardcavan. It was opened in 1959 and is located on the same site as the first Wexford bridge, built in 1795. A Company had been formed in 1794 to build two bridges, one spanning the Slaney at Wexford, the other further up-river at Ferrycarrig.

Cornelius Grogan of Johnstown Castle and other leading citizens of the time including two prominent local landowners, Bagenal Harvey and John Henry Colclough, were all executed on Wexford Bridge for their part in the 1798 rebellion. Many of the other subscribers to the bridge also lost their lives when it was used as a place of execution for prisoners on both sides of the political divide.

The contract for the bridge was awarded to Lemuel Cox, an engineer from Boston, who completed it in 1795. Wexford bridge was made of American oak and was 1,554ft long and 34ft wide, with seventy-five piers of oak driven into the river bed. It had a drawbridge to allow ships with masts to pass. It was elegantly adorned with Chinese railings from end to end.

A portion of the bridge collapsed in 1827 but it was quickly repaired as it was a toll bridge. It became a toll-free bridge in 1851 and was replaced by the bridge at Carcur in 1856. The older bridge was demolished in 1866. The 'New Bridge' as it is known in Wexford had to undergo major remedial work in 1997. *(Image from the John Scanlon collection courtesy of Dominic Kiernan)*

THIS CURRENT BRIDGE is one of the main access routes to the town and is an essential part of the panorama of Wexford. The 1858 bridge further up the river was demolished but the buttresses are still intact and clearly visible today at Wexford Harbour Boat Club and at the opposite side of the river.

WEXFORD COURTHOUSE

THE BUILDING IN the right-hand foreground was Wexford Courthouse, which stood on Commercial Quay facing the foot of Wexford Bridge.

The courthouse was built in 1805 to replace an earlier courthouse in the Bullring. It was designed by Sir Richard Morrison who was also responsible for Wexford Jail and the County Hall. As can be seen, it was a substantial and imposing building. Its recessed façade had two projecting wings and there were four Doric columns in the main entrance. Records show that continuous alterations had to be made to the building and even with this work completed neither the judges nor the general public were satisfied with the accommodation. In 1863, major plans were put in place to enlarge and refurbish the building. Detailed plans of the inside of the courthouse are extant from this date.

The Grand Juries and Board of Guardians were replaced by County Councils in 1898.

On 22 April 1899 Wexford County Council met for the first time in the grand jury room in Wexford Courthouse. The first chairman was Sir Thomas Henry Grattan Esmonde and the vice-chairman was Mr Edmond Hore. The courthouse was to be home to Wexford County Council until September 1920. The courthouse was destroyed by an explosion and fire on 18 June 1921 during the War of Independence. *(Image from the Lawrence collection courtesy of the National Library of Ireland)*

TODAY THE SITE of the former Courthouse is a car park. Despite occupying such a prominent position in the town it has not been developed for major commercial use.

WEXFORD
UNION
WORKHOUSE

THE DERELICT BUILDING on an elevated site overlooking the town seen on the left of the photograph was, until 1992, Wexford County Hospital; prior to that it had served as Wexford Union Workhouse. The building, dating from 1842, was designed to a standard plan by architect George Wilkinson and was to accommodate 600 occupants. By 1845, 290 people had been admitted.

The Great Famine had a devastating effect on the whole country. While Wexford town escaped the worst ravages of the famine as experienced in other parts of the country, it did impact on the labouring and cottier classes. The on-going agricultural depression meant that admissions to the workhouse continued to increase, reaching 1,000 by 1848. The aftermath of the famine resulting in continued depravation for the agricultural classes, which meant that the numbers in the Workhouse did not decline for many years.

The main three-storey building in the centre housed the Master's quarters and the male and female quarters were

housed at each side. A single-storey building at the rear of the main block contained the bakery, washroom, infirmary, chapel and dining hall.

In 1872, the Sisters of St John of God community began to work in the infirmary of the Workhouse. They continued to work there when the new Wexford County Hospital took over the building in 1920. *(Image from the John Scanlon collection courtesy of Dominic Kiernan)*

THE MAIN BUILDING has been derelict since the County Hospital moved to a new site nearby in 1992. A preservation order was placed on the building but there seems to be little interest in restoring it. The new building in front of the old hospital is the Farnogue Health Facility, which opened in 2013.

YMCA HALL

THIS PHOTOGRAPH SHOWS three significant buildings on North Main Street. In the foreground on the right is the YMCA Hall, beside it is Whites Hotel and on the left is the offices of the *Wexford Independent*. White's Hotel is treated as a separate article (see pp. 94-95).

This building provided premises for the Young Men's Christian Association (YMCA) in Wexford for 140 years. Founded in London in 1844, the YMCA was part of a worldwide organisation which aimed to put Christian principles into practice by developing a healthy mind, body and spirit. The Wexford YMCA was founded by Revd Richard Waddy Elgee, rector of Wexford and provided social and recreational activities for the young people of the Protestant community. The building was constructed by Edwin Thomas Willis in 1861. The interior is impressive, with an imposing central staircase and a number of rooms for theatrical productions, billiards, table tennis, badminton and reading. There is a large function room on the first floor. To the left of the main entrance is the original entrance for carriages to White's Hotel.

The premises on the left of the photograph, displaying a distinctive globe-like sign, was the offices of the *Wexford Independent*. It was edited by John Greene and was first published in 1830. It was in this newspaper that James Fintan Lalor first advocated fair rent, free trade and fixity of tenure. Greene was a local politician and served seven terms as Mayor of Wexford. He died in 1890 and the paper ceased publication in 1906. *(Image from the Lawrence collection courtesy of the National Library of Ireland)*

THE YMCA BUILDING was sold in 2000 to a local businessman who was sensitive to the architecture of the building and it currently houses the Vine Restaurant upstairs and Fusion Café on the ground floor. The offices of the *Wexford Independent* are long gone and are now shops.

WHITE'S HOTEL

THE NEW WHITE'S Hotel dominates Abbey Street. The street gets its name from Selskar Abbey nearby. The medieval town wall, with a circular mural tower, runs along one side of the street behind the houses on the left-hand side of the photograph. Originally it was known as Market Street as it linked Cornmarket to Selskar Abbey and then it curved around the abbey and ended at Westgate. The row of houses dating from the early nineteenth century on the left-hand side of the street was removed in the 1970s and sections of the wall have been restored.

White's Hotel founded in 1779 by John White has been an integral part of the economic, cultural and social life of Wexford town for over 200 years. In the early 1800s it became a Coaching Inn when Charles Bianconi established his stage-coach network.

White's incorporated an earlier house, owned by the Wheelock family, which was the birthplace of Robert McClure, best known as an arctic explorer and the first white man to traverse the North West Passage in 1854. He was knighted by Queen Victoria. As the town prospered in the nineteenth century the Hotel expanded. Among its famous guests in 1919 was the Crown Prince of Saudi Arabia, Faisal Ibn Saud, who was guest of the Wexford solicitor, James O'Connor, while on a shooting holiday on the North Slob. *(Image from the John Scanlon collection courtesy of Dominic Kiernan)*

IN THE TWENTIETH century the Hotel came into possession of the McCarthy family who owned and managed it until 1997. The hotel had expanded onto Abbey Street with a large collection of modern buildings in the 1970s. Due to economic difficulties in the late 1980s the business had to scale back and part of the Hotel was converted into a library from 1987 to 1999. In 1997, Michael Burke purchased White's Hotel and in January 2004 closed the Hotel to embark on a major redevelopment. The hotel reopened in June 2006, unveiling the all new White's of Wexford. The rebuilding of White's Hotel has meant that the reception and other main services now front onto Abbey Street rather than the Main Street. The dramatic projecting portico on the street has caused controversy as it is in stark contrast to the surrounding area which includes Selskar Abbey and the medieval town wall.

BIBLIOGRAPHY

Bassett, G., *Wexford County: Guide and Directory* (Dublin, 1885)

Berney, M., *Centenary Record of the Twin Churches in Wexford* (Wexford, 1958)

Colfer, B., *Wexford a Town and its Landscape* (Cork, 2008)

Coulter, B. and F., www.wexfordharbour.ie

De Vál, S.S., *Churches of the Diocese of Ferns* (Wexford, 2004)

Enright, M., *Men of Iron* (Wexford, 1987)

Furlong, N. and J. Hayes, *County Wexford in the Rare Oul' Times*, 5v (Wexford, 1985-2010)

Grattan-Flood, W.H., *History of the Diocese of Ferns* (Waterford, 1916)

Griffiths, G., *Chronicles of County Wexford to 1877* (Enniscorthy, 1877)

Hore, P.H., *History of the Town and County of Wexford*, 6v (London, 1900-1911)

Journal of the Wexford Historical Society 23v (1968-2012)

Lacy, T., *Sights and Scenes in our Fatherland* (London, 1863)

Murphy, H., *Families of County Wexford* (Dublin, 1986)

The Past, the organ of the Uí Cinsealaigh Historical Society 31v (1920-2012)

Rossiter, N., *Wexford Port – A History* (Wexford, 1989)

— *Wexford a History, a Tour and a Miscellany* (Dublin, 2005)

— *My Wexford* (Wexford, 2006)

— *Streets of Wexford* (Dublin, 2009)

— *Remembering Wexford* (2010)

Rowe, D. and Wilson, C. (eds), *High Skies-low Lands: An Anthology of the Wexford Slobs and Harbour* (Enniscorthy, 1996)

Scallan, E., *The Twin Churches* (Wexford, 2008)